DEAR OCTOBER

DEAR OCTOBER

POEMS

Mary Morris

TEXAS REVIEW PRESS ~ HUNTSVILLE, TEXAS

Published by Texas Review Press
Huntsville, Texas 77341
texasreviewpress.org

Printed in the United States of America

Library of Congress Cataloging in Publication Data
    is on file at the Library of Congress, Washington, DC

Cover photograph: Autumn capture of Dark Hedges, Co Antrim,
    © Stephen Emerson

For my mother

Table of Contents

Late November

It's the closest we have ever been—
slipping off my jeans, sliding into the shower

with my mother, washing the galaxy
of her back scattered with planets.

Once, she carried me behind that tumor,
emptied her milk into my mouth.

The body remembers what is primal.
I dress and feed her, brush her hair.

Outside, three bronze leaves
suspend from the ash. My mother and I

lie down, fragrant with soap, curled
as embryos. Later we wake

like lovers, our bodies spooned.

My Mother Arranges the Manger

with rolls of cotton snow.
I am ten, playing the piano.

Wise men at the far right bear
frankincense, gold, myrrh.

The legs of the lone sheep
are restored with toothpicks.

A bent halo attaches to the back
of our Messiah by a wire.

I fire off Bach's *Ode to Joy*.
The Nativity scene trembles.

I play over voices in the house—
a fugue for Billy, *adagio*

for the baby, boogie-woogie
for papa. I press my foot

on the loud pedal as holiness
reverberates. I am a god here

with my small hands, long fingers,
reading the code of music.

Her Mouth

is an ocean. Her breathing,
a storm at sea. My mother

is having a tooth pulled today.
This sweet tooth she has had

since she skipped from her tenement
to buy strawberry ice cream

for her parents, running
home before it melted.

That same molar bit into rations
during poverty in war

and through the feathery
wedding cake her mother baked.

One eyetooth drew blood
from the flesh of a midwife's arm.

El otro diente, another tooth
cracked on an apple last week.

One by one, my mother is losing
all of her teeth. Now I understand

what this means:
someday she won't be hungry.

Dear December,

A billion flakes of silence—

rice in the wedding of sky.
I shatter the mirrored pond of ice

where air stings and husky toads
sleep under the weight of it all.

I miss them and the bull snakes
touring the land, the land where

the sea green chair becomes
a lost temple in the sun

among waves of snowdrifts.
The yucca are frozen

anemone. The sage, owl skulls.
Junipers are thickened

with flickers, pear trees stripped
to skeletons, their fingers

pointing in all directions.

Second Visit from Hospice

Before the social worker exits the house
she takes me aside, hands me a paper sack

for end of life: droppers and vials of morphine.
Place it in the back of your refrigerator,

she says, before asking if my mother has
funeral plans. I know them all, down to the plot

where she will accordion next to my father.
Then a force emerges through the floors,

slaps handprints on walls, thwack sounds
resembling passports being stamped.

I understand, the social worker declares
as she closes the door behind her.

Clouds form in the attic, billow
down the stairs, and I know my father

is here. Nevertheless, the angel of death
rests its head on my mother's shoulder,

says *not yet*, not yet. If you find yourself
eating plums by the window and see a ghost

under a tree, report it. Your comments
will be added to the Roster of Weeping

inside the Library of Absolute Missing.
Delicate business, these visits down under.

How the dead unearth, make claim again.

Toulouse-Lautrec, a Café in Paris

There is something to be said for aging
if you have some wild passion to replace it

as Lautrec did, painting on the avenue
near the Moulin Rouge.

And if you can capture light, embed it
into your skull, practice and eat voraciously

the power of skill and beauty,
then it doesn't matter so much—

the skin and bones sliding out
underneath you as you age, the trapeze

of the body forever slipping
from this circus of the living

as you praise breath
in its vanishing.

Dear January,

Old Moon, Ice Moon,
you rotate your bare shoulder.

Eclipsed with resolutions,
you make the Wolf Moon howl

while we freeze. How can we
suffer toward sap, wondering

when we may climb out
of darkness, heavily

swathed and cursing you?
The trees are diseased.

The elk, few. We forgive you
January, ask for provisions,

for these bodies to be spared—
our own and those who passion us

with their skin song in these arctic
nights at the hearth. Hear us.

We are making sacrifices.

Deduction

My mother says, *You know the person*
who brings the uterus on Sunday?

Ma, they took your uterus.
Nearly five decades ago

following ten acts of childbirth
a surgeon closed her womb.

No more bodies coming through her.
No more bearing down. *Honey,*
you know, what is it called? Uterus?

My mother, victor of crosswords,
is deeply concerned, her head
bent over her chest as she searches

for the word on the shelves
of her temporal lobe.
Ah, Eucharist, I say. *Yes.*

And she thanks me, her interpreter
in the country called forgetfulness,

her guide through the nation of memory.

Dear February,

Month of the Gray Storm Moon
Behind Cloud, at the center of winter

we follow tracks, blood in the snow,
deer dancers from San Juan Pueblo.

On their backs, russet fans
of turkey feathers. Antlered heads.

James says his tribe journeys south
from the mountain at sunrise

as the day opens its bleeding
eye, splits the sky. Turtle rattles

quick-start bonfire, gold strobe
for the cold to warm us.

Hunters cross crescent bows, release
arrows through four directions.

The children, fawns, rest their heads
against their fathers' legs.

One hundred and fifty Tewa singers
chant, embodying the deer.

The kiva, a prayer book
we enter and exit.

The Place Where It Escapes

Jung's interpretation of losing teeth
in a dream is synonymous with

loosening a grip
on the unconscious.

Freud, of course, believed
it had something to do with castration.

In primitive belief, a hole in the skull
is the place where the soul escapes.

If you swallow your teeth
are you trying your best to keep them,

an attempt to preserve yourself,
remain cognizant, store power

in the dark underbody of organs?
My mother used to say,

*If you swallow that seed
a tree gonna grow inside your belly.*

If she swallows teeth in her sleep
will she cultivate a body?

Maternal

One cold early morning, my mother wore
a red scarf on her head, led the panting bird dog
inside, nails clicking the brown linoleum floor
until the hound curled into a pile of old towels.

It was the dog's fourth litter. She worked
hard that winter, delivering numerous quail,
duck, geese, and turkey at my father's
and brothers' feet. Eight puppies born

in two hours. One stillborn. She licked
their sealed eyes and slick bodies,
ate the glistening dark afterbirth
while they squealed. *She's lost too much*

blood, my mother said. *Not enough milk.*
So she took two old rubber gloves, filled them
with warm cow's milk, poked holes
in the fingertips. We held them up

for the puppies to suck. All were hushed
as we gathered round, gaped at them, and then
went out to play. It was early spring, after all.
The grass green. Lilacs just beginning to bloom.

I Try to Get Out of the Way
So the Soul May Draw Near

—but I keep tripping on steps in the earth
get lost in my mother's skirts

and then it approaches, without
hatred and cares, with grace,

ice in the mouth,
pleasure of green.

It digs its way deep
akin to a man burying his best friend,

the yellow finches working their way
into the canals of my ears

where they enter the heart
nest in the solar plexus

and I am born
once again.

Hymn No. 34, Do Not Resuscitate

The forewarning, held by magnets
on the outside of a refrigerator
filled with sustenance:

milk, eggs, fruit, leftover
omelet, and morphine
drops. Our daily reminder

she is still here. Warm
and cared for, cleansed
and fed.

Our evening prayer evolves
as squall of bronze leaves
crackle through an open door.

Her breath diminished
in the sacristy of lungs.
Astringent. Torn asunder.

Do not resuscitate.
Refuse to force the soul
back into the body.

He Says March

and I think pomegranate, midnight,
crystallized silver leaves, the night shift

of snow and darkness, a film noir.
I think tree carcasses,

vines in their scrim of glass.
Ice-gauzed, mouth of a sky gone

agape. Dear March, writer of elegies
that keeps changing its mind—

sound of a great horned owl,
a stand of horses in sleet

vexed with their drizzled coats—
the ruins of winter—gray rubble.

In the eddy, leaf decay, stick tangle,
baring fossil under glaciers

blinking away. Dear Crust Moon,
Chaste Moon, and yes, Death Moon,

I say, give it up. Give it up
for spring—daylight, saving time.

Cherry Blossom Festival

Spring trees embrace fists of white flowers.
A gust of wind and it's snowing blossoms.

Branches sway, dip in water, like a woman
leaning in to wash her long hair.

Pink petals explode into fireworks called
girl spilling a basket of corollas

or obscured by clouds at sunset.
Perhaps *meteor showers in April.*

I think of *Shinto, the spirit's homecoming*
of her—an empty kimono.

Drowned memories in the tongues of rain.
The way we arrive here

from a distant land
to a tea ceremony on the lawn.

Heritage

After my parents divorced
my mother took a trip to Ireland
to be held by her feet by some stocky men

and lowered upside down
so that she could face the dark, kiss
the Blarney Stone, and move on.

She brought me an Irish sweater
still hanging in my closet. A ghost of wool.
Stories of selkies. Scent of earthy stew.

Her parents, Black Irish, Donegal
descendants, lived with us. On Saint
Patrick's Day, under the spell of corned

beef cabbage and fast fiddle music,
we danced, while my grandpa told first
the legend of a saint who drove snakes

out of the country of our blood, then
the story of famine, ships, passengers
thrown overboard into the icy Atlantic.

Years later, when they were gone,
my mother discovered she was adopted
and we weren't Irish at all,

but French. Blue damask,
Napoleon's soldiers crossing
the Seine at dusk.

Song

For the past year, perplexed, my mother asks
if I hear music. She says melodies haunt her.
Yesterday, big band. Today, gospel.

In the beginning I wondered, *Is it
the thin membrane to the other side?*
And maybe it is. Or possibly she is preparing,

or fate is composing its final deliverance hymn.
It's just like her, in the middle of an audio book
on a subject like *The History of India*

in the 1800s, falling asleep, mouth agape,
while a rosary slips through her arthritic fingers
between sheets of blue madras and tamarind leaves.

She mumbles about the scent of red saffron,
humming a raga in what sounds like Sanskrit:
Vishnu, Ganga, Kushmanda. Tonight my mother

holds a skull cup, says she possesses
jars of blood and honey. She rides a tiger,
re-creates the world, has become a deity.

Autobiographía Religioso

after Frank O'Hara

When I was a child, I pretended to be a priest
and fashioned Communion from coins of bread.

I practiced on my younger brothers
all five of them, even the baby.

This is my body. This is my blood.

My mother caught me once
and scolded me for being sacrilegious,

so I never told her that my older sister
was hearing confessions

and we had to say, *Bless me,
for we have sinned*

before repenting to *Her Grace,*
for she was a Bishop.

Dear April,

The wind, an adolescent, bows the violin,
blows the doors open.

A blizzard of apple blossoms
litters your feet, softens

the undergrowth
born face up, baptized by the light.

Awakening Moon, Jade, Grass,
and Egg Moon—let us

draw a little map in the dirt,
a plot to plant our seeds again.

Channel water from the mountains
through the fields.

Easter

The thin river below
winds through villages
and rows of maize

where weathered crosses
and *descansos*
border the road.

We are headed
to the tamale stand
where Señora Sanchez
assembles them—

the corn blue as sky,
the chile red
as saint's blood.

Birth

I was born during the Year of the Snake
on an oil field in the seventh house

under the sign of Cancer.
One of twelve—every night

dinner was the Last Supper.
Who were Peter, Matthew,

Luke, and John? Brothers.
Where was Judas? Troubled,

in the field hunting rabbits.
The rooster crowed three times.

I discovered near the stable
a horned toad someone had nailed

to the ground. *Easter. Pilate.*
I called Dial-a-Saint, prayed

to Mary-at-the-Station
who the announcer said

could broadcast to heaven.

Matías

My brother lives on the edge of town,
the fray, just past the airport. He built a house

of mud over brontosaurus bones.
A place where wild pigs and donkeys roam.

Where feral cats come, mewing for milk
as they are stroked by this man, my brother

who resembles St. Francis, who has been martyred
thirty-six times between New England

and New Mexico. My brother's house
is his temple. Cats wrap around his ankles.

He cleans his own teeth. Within his memory
lives an oak tree under a pristine blue sky.

He made a house in that enormous deciduous
sentry over a pond. Water that ached

into a mud puddle during a drought.
He wanted to move out of our home,

live in his tree, be a leaf, the always-observer
while he waited for our father's pink car

to arrive so he could teach my brother
a lesson. My brother, extremely resourceful,

knew all the best, secret hiding places.
My mother wore lipstick and an apron,

created casseroles generous with cheese.

She had more than nine children. We bathed

three at a time. My brother waited
all his life to read. In the meantime,

he painted self-portraits like Van Gogh.
He painted himself against an Oklahoma

sunset, reminding us of an apocalypse.
He possessed magic, could walk on his hands,

jump on the water with trick skis.
One night he woke us from our sleep

during the great tornado of 1967
and we followed him safely through

rain to the flooded storm cellar.
He could jump off a bridge, swim under water,

reappear in the next town, fake a limp,
and get a ride back home. My brother

has Graves' disease. If there were a cure
called back from the grave,

he could reenact the miracle of Lazarus.
Amen. Amen. Good God, Amen.

Dear May, First Hummingbird

Iridescent green, like a Christmas ornament
we packed away last season.

Little Flame of summer,
who has flown all the way

from South America, for blossoms
in my garden in the desert—crimson,

blue salvia, cups of penstemon.
Feel the chill loosen, melt of winter.

Astonished by the vigor of a pocket-sized
body, hovering over the edge of nectar.

Keeper of the season,
little whirlwind at my window.

All winter I have waited for you
among the dry leaves aligned with wolf spiders.

Here, under the Flower Moon, Hare Globe, Grass
and Planting Sphere—

Weather Alert

One brother is out frog-gigging.
Five are with the dogs hunting.
The wind drives west.

Sky turns midnight blue at two.
My sister's freckles are black seeds,
her mouth, a rose, opens before she screams.

There are sightings.
We tie things down. The raft.
The cellar—flooded

though there has been no rain.
Rats swim the surface.
Our Lady of Water, hold back.

Tarantulas migrate from Mexico,
move swiftly their hairiness.
In its initiation, wind whispers relief.

We get drunk from its coolness.
The days, effervescent—a mist
of heat lightning surrounds us.

Sometimes a channel of air,
an amalgam, pulls everything together,
then blows apart. My sister runs

through mint, a troubadour of scent.
I slip inside to the grotto of our house,
keep playing piano keys, Chopin

sharp. My sanctuary—I am the only person
allowed to play piano in the living room
with family portraits: Uncle Isaac,

Aunt Nina. All are oblivious
to my privilege. When the sheet music
says *staccato*, I think *stigmata*.

Cutting My Mother's Hair

Scalp, visible enough—
I'm careful not to cut too much.

My mother's hair,
from dark to gray,

from luxurious to frayed—
wisps of a cloud passing.

A halo in the light,
for she loved and labored

and bore us. God, may her end
be ethereal and painless.

Tempest

Over us, a plague of addiction.
Saint Martin in the corner says, *Give*
me your tired, your sorrows, afflictions.

He is east of an echo. And three years older.
You can hear him over the cicadas, the storm
bleeding beyond all alphabets,

language in your pockets,
above the crow, horned toads, and egret,
through the sound of gurgling water,

a house with aquarium, producing oxygen,
freshwater tropical, prophecies
unfolding. The funnel, nonnegotiable

tunnel from purgatory. A channel
of tongues. Can't you taste the candy?
Danger and pleasure. Whoever

you thought you were—now the horses
are swimming in air. The dark sky
replaces the ceiling swinging with lamps—

the world, a tempest of verbs.
Whoever you were—alas,
there is climate and deconstruction.

There will be holy water and mud.
There will be miracles to follow.

Dear June, Summer Solstice

Night pours out half its beaker
while day fills our chalice of light.

Measured. Rose Moon. Planting orb.
Old ghosts of winter whisk away, straw

stuck between their teeth, bedraggled
in their 17th-century pointed hats.

Dark hive—hexagonal, paper-celled,
waxed and honeyed. Whir

of a single hummingbird in the mouth
of a blue delphinium.

Claim it—the North Pole tilted
toward the sun as this land receives

the degree of its deepest radiance.
Shadows withdraw while we convert

prayer bead to seed, witness gauze of gnats
blur above an orchard of apricot trees.

At night, under a Honey Moon
we suck the rose flesh of watermelon

while dusty dogs roll in their sleep
through Whitman blades of emerald green.

Nuevo México

This is the land of *duende*.

Penitentes erect crosses on hills,
whip themselves beyond arroyos—

air dry enough, land hard enough
to grow thorns on cactus for the crown of Jesus.

Flamenco dancers stamp their feet
in dark corners of smoky bars.

In every village on Sunday you are offered
to eat and drink the body and blood of Christ.

Amethyst mountains rise luminous—
nine thousand feet of pulled sediment.

Crone

This year my mother has swallowed teeth
in her sleep, wakes with new sensations—

smooth, empty sockets in place of molars.
She frowns in the mirror, says, *Pumpkin face*.

But this afternoon she had the remainder
of her incisors extracted and now

really does look aged, lips drawn in
like an illustration of a crone in a fairytale,

an old woman her grandchildren adore.
Crone, a word tied to magic, reduced

to malicious, hag, cantankerous
from *carrion*. Raised to wise heroine.

Namesake

after Jimi Hendrix

In Catechism I learn that once
I was a virgin visited by a large angel
heaving wings the size of a small airplane.

Gabriel. An explosion of a thousand tiny
honeysuckle blossoms outside my window.
White perfume.

But I am also Mary Magdalene and see
the other part of him—a man whose eyes
turn gold as amber from the Dead Sea
with his love for me, whose compass
of desire points feverishly

flush toward my map of exotic orchards
lined with date palms, trees saturated with figs.
He becomes sated, drenched, quivering
in the waters of my Hebrew heart.

When my mother repeats my name, I dream
I am part of a rosary, *Hail Mary, Mother
of God*, fingering scented beads
of sandalwood or tiny spheres of blue glass.

Hail Mary, full of grace.

The Lord is with thee, she says. She says,
"Maria, you skipped confession again, and
if you ever have an abortion, don't tell me."
I won't, but my sister will.

Blessed art thou amongst women, and blessed
is the fruit of thy womb, Jesus.

I leave home. On the highway to my Future
Queendom. I carry a backpack with the quiver
of Saint Sebastian's arrows. Around my feet,
Roman sandals. My first ride, a '69 Mustang

chariot. The driver, a young man, wears a halo
of hair. Draped around the mirror are blue
African trade beads. On the tape deck,
the voice of Jimi Hendrix shines seductive
and lucid as the June Moon.

And the wind whispers Mary.

Moving to Santa Fe

I packed my boxes, beat the tornado.
My brother followed in his truck
with my bed and books of photos.

Good-bye father and mother, seven
brothers who fed us wild animals.
Farewell to the stone house strangled

with red dirt, rose rocks,
green hills, and burnt grass.
I will miss you, armadillos

and hairy hands of tarantulas
crossing the road in the dark.
Farewell friends. I'm not far.

Visit me in my mud house
under the shadow of the mesa.
Bring me peaches.

Dear July,

Hot clouds, matchbox air, smolder.
Pontormo blue. Chiaroscuro.

Mead and rose steeped in heat.
Nectarines, sexy and fragrant.

A chandelier of peaches suspended
above our table. We hunger the banquet

our devotion feeds us, sleep under
a Thunder Moon, Buck Moon,

new velvet antler of Deer
and fresh-cut Hay Moon—

Wake to morning sparrows.
Matins.

Living at 7,000 Feet

Some of us live in a fable
of piñon trees and mushroom rings
falling asleep in the day.

It's the altitude, they say. Or attitude
but just the same, it's lightheaded
and multiplies while tourists drink tequila.

Try filing your taxes while steeped in a fairytale,
an apple orchard fragrant as an entire arboretum
while a crone holds out a blood-red fruit to you

as you overhear a priest give a sermon
from a pulpit on the salvation of war
while hexing *aborto*.

Picture the fear of god and witches,
Curanderas in charming adobe villages.
Imagine potions—elixirs,

gnarled *oshá* root, and dandelion,
milkweed, and thistle
brewed with aromatics.

Pennyroyal, sage, and lavender
issued with the sign of the cross,
sacred dirt, and holy water.

Sovereign

If what Rilke says is true, that *poetry*
is the past that breaks out in our hearts,
I can see her now, and there's that slit
that rips into, restores memory.

She's up past our curfews, knits blue
sweaters, nibbles on pretzels, sips
a Coors baby eight, television
flickering on her face.

She stood guard at her red chair
for 24 years as her children stumbled
in from their games, dates,
concerts, bars, and bodegas

and at times during the war
when it used to be shown
on television where she searched
the screen of a jungle for a son.

If she ever noticed us drunk, stoned,
or ravished by a late-night date,
or father with his reek of scotch
fresh from sleeping

with his secretary, she never said.
My mother, sovereign ruler
of our little nation, our low-lying
broken country of dreams.

Her Second Call for Sacrament of the Sick

When she feels her soul is in danger
my mother arranges for
the courier of her savior.

Before Father Frank enters the house
she has laboriously dressed, smoothed on
her coral lipstick, and taken inventory.

She will first confess her sins,
though sharply adds, she hasn't had
much opportunity to offend.

The priest hears her trespasses,
delivers absolution. *In the name
of the Father, the Son.* We hold hands

as Father anoints her through saints
of his own choosing. *In the name
of Augustine, Saint Mary Magdalene,*

Theresa, and Valentine. Remember,
he reminds us, *Jesus sat at the table
with the poor, the blind, and addicted.*

As soon as the priest exits,
my mother reaches for a cigarette.
I feel transformed, she says.

*Now I can smoke, sit at the window,
listen for birds.* Soon, mourning
doves coo on the sill in sunlight

reminding us of the Holy Ghost.
For now, my mother's illness
has been misdiagnosed.

Dear August,

Warmer than a teahouse
on the equator—

Lightning Moon,
tempest builder,

we search for a storm cellar
while the fist of God breaks

through the sound barrier.
Come, come, sweet shelter.

The Book I Am Writing

begins in the South
and ends in New Mexico.
It's a litany of addiction
with the penitent brother and the benevolent mother.
It's clever with little rhymes
and an epic poem taking its time.
There is heavy impasto of suffering
and a lifting from the *Joy of Man's Desiring.*
There are relinquished choices
that will risk everything. And nothing.
Inside is a child with a fever and one who reads backward.
I had a brain hemorrhage once, so there's that.
And there's that mother and her daughter
playing all-night Scrabble, a mosaic
of a story chaotic as any home.
I believe the success of a family is how you survive it.
I believed in the book of truth,
that the last chapter would be titled "Death at the Station,"
but the book I am writing begins with an elegy
and ends in genesis.

Invitation to My House

Roll the globe starward,
stroll the Plaza of Immaculata,
eat dust on Calle Santo Niño,
cross the field of sparrows,
pass the magician riding
his horse along the furrows.
Forget waterfalls. This is high
mountain desert. Pass the yucca,
sideline the grove of Russian Olive.

Enter a green-winged gate
through lavender and basil.
Find the house with windows
set in mud, radiant and futuristic
for the moment. Remove your shoes
while I wash the dust from your feet,
give you well water cool to drink.

Coyote

Let's have a quick game of Scrabble, my mother says,
as it becomes late afternoon. I am thinking of the sun
going down and the darkness coming on, walking
home down the road. About the coyote in my arroyo

and the cloudy sky, but already she has poured
out her letters, contemplating her squares of phonemes
to activate into words and strategize for double scores.

As if the night were made of Scrabble—a small bag
of letters spilling from heaven while we decide
who will begin, have the advantage or disadvantage
over the other.

When my mother and I play this game, it's an alliance,
the board becoming territory we claim with words
or lands where we must coexist.

She turns my *pastures* to *failure.* I pull *marsupial*
out of her *proboscis, leech* from *sommelier.* She
gives me *perilous*—a triple word score—while I
strike through, twice with *exodus,* then *exempt.*

We break, eat a soup of fish and leeks.
In the center of the table, a bowl of fruit
with shiny lemon and pomegranates. Above,
a wall of crosses picked up along the way.

We share biscochitos, bite into anise seeds
as they release their sweet licorice,
and I am sure we are both thinking
of our given syllables.

Last month I admitted my mother to the hospital
with a broken hip, her face distorted in pain
as I fed her by hand, spooned the soft applesauce
through the hungry port of her mouth.
My patient, my mother, my child.

We return to the game, tally the score, which is even.
I give her the gesture that I must leave, while she
looks back with her cello-eye bowing those low
deep notes of not wanting me to go.

Walking home in the dark below constellations, I hear
contagious yips of coyotes who discover their prey
filling the arroyos. I imagine wild beasts
with mangy coats. Those standing

in the middle of the road in daylight
the other day bravely staking out new territory.
Getting used to humans, the neighbor said.
I had to clap and yell before they'd slink away.

One stayed. And tonight I feel as if my mother
and I live in the old country of wolves and winter,
fur and teeth.

The Enemy Becomes More Dangerous

After you lose your hair
I make fetishes with fur,
note the shape of your skull.

We must feed you, conquer cells
that multiply, prepare the port again,
sail the venom to bring you home.

Chemo, the great destroyer—
Shiva, standing with one foot
above our world.

Rumors

The morning my mother told me my sister had cancer
I forgave her.

One cannot listen to the devil looking over
your shoulder, saying, *guilty, guilty* forever.

Boredom never existed.
There were always others.

I played "Moon River" on the piano.
Then Otis Redding.

My mother's daughters swam in a lake
bubbly as champagne

from a beach where geologists discovered
human remains.

Each of us will remember
events under water.

In the day, we did our chores, fed dogs, horses.
Stirred the pot, washed dishes, swept floors.

At night, the family was a party
of alcohol and hats, whistle and song.

Then more alcohol, fewer hats.

Sometimes my sister and I slept on top
of each other to keep ourselves warm.

Dear September,

I drove away
from the news of the world,

its gaped mouth, oil refinery, bullet teeth,
tongue hoary with greed.

I want the moon and I want it hallowed
for it is late September

and the flowers are all papery
like gold tissue confetti quivering in wind.

I drove away, the blossoms of chamisa
releasing their bullion, sprays of purple

aster lining the road.
Once again we have reappeared in autumn

at our carved Spanish doors, behind portals
staring into the light.

Desire

Everything I was aware of
I desired to write about.

To be reintroduced, returned to
again—when we were women.

To interpret like a palm reader
or seer. To weigh the future

against the past. To find one's
bearings as constellations for sailors.

As benediction. To remember.
Memorize the roosting places

of scissor-tailed flycatchers, or catch
silence before the yellow twister

funneled toward us, about to eat
everything in its path, sucking us up

with all the shingles from the roof.
To remember our pony, Sunshine,

bundling himself, holding ground
against the wind.

In a Book Called Sisters

Father builds our room to share,
mother sews curtains, blankets of vines.
Emerald, where pink roses climb
in feathered sleep piped with thorns.

Father builds beds against the wall,
permanent, with hidden drawers.
One above each where memories are
stored, spun into dreams.

Underneath, shelves pull out to become
doll houses where we place Kotex
for their beds, a blue towel for a pool.
How we might want the world at eight.

During adolescence, we are in a book
called *War and Peace*, open to a chapter
of summer, scent of honeysuckle,
unbolted windows, crawl from them

at midnight, meet boyfriends.
In the seventeenth chapter you marry—
a virgin with a dowry, own thirty
pairs of shoes. Before I smoke a leaf

out the bathroom window, I play
piano and you dance. There is another
language between sisters—
what binds and what divides.

And the way illness revises us.
The way our mother, hooked up
to her oxygen tank, can't find
the words *au revoir*.

When the Night Is Still Damp with Dreams

and dogs howl at wild beasts outside your window—
when you lie naked under the gray cloud
of a comforter, where you remember the elk
that appeared in the one spot of sun in the meadow
while trout jumped in the river behind you,

you will know
what grows between,
what pact you can agree on
with the angel of a brief appearance—
your life, place of your husk, testament on earth.

When you take in god notes, voices—
before the drowning sound
between water, salt, and air—

that muscle of a lost baptism
into a novena, salve, grotto
of the bandaged eye you transcend.

Heaven

You won't need a password
or be required to identify

your name, gender, race,
religion, or political party.

You will be transparent.
Birds will fly through you.

Black Mesa

There are mountains above us   thirsty and powerful.
They cause the lungs to labor and eyes to dry.

And there are garnets inside   arteries of caves beyond
up against cliffs of the Río Grande   at the river's bend

where mayfly hatch   and rainbow trout rise,
but it's the mesas I am more intimate with—

suspended in the middle of sky with their tabletop views
endless horizon   vermillion sunset peeling back the dark

as it reveals the zodiac   Jupiter and Mars
where we search for satellites   godlike

with their single eyes   collecting data
before they disappear into earth's shadow.

The Art of Dying

There are cravings we hunger for, savor,
are gratified with, left wanting all over again—

the body waxing and waning,
exhausted and restored.

Once, you hid secrets, veils in private drawers—
now you can disappear.

I Called the Birds Scissors

so I could feel her fear of all winged beings.
The way she slips from her great intellect.

Oh! she trembles when we sit outside
as a tanager flies by. *Achh!* she shrieks

as a sparrow skitters close to our feet.
I could grasp it, turning my hands into a nest

or a cage. I could show her how
quiet and harmless, how vulnerable

with its shaking feathers, like her—
then let it go.

Dear October,

First last wish: *To see the aspens*
turn gold one last time.

Tonight, a Hunter's Moon
above the Sangre de Cristo Mountains.

Blood and Grain and Fox Moon—
we depart in the morning.

Let's go. *I can't. Too stiff*
to get dressed. At daybreak

I brace my body, carry my mother
to the car in nightgown and slippers.

We are on her last ride climbing up—
suspense of a roller coaster.

Yellow flashes in the sunlight
of leaves in transition—we are in heaven.

My mother is looking down at the world
of miniature people, their mud houses

and infinitesimally small cars
as they drive on their little roads

where she has already been.

About Dear October

These poems were written during the last years of my mother's life. Without realizing it at the time, they were often the way I prepared for losing her—through events, memories, landscapes, and dreams. Frequently, in those last years, my mother and I would lie in her bed, holding, sometimes gripping hands. The act of caring for her was not always simple or easy, yet often it was incredibly intimate and beautiful.

Mary Morris

Notes

Names of the moons are drawn from various cultures around the world.

"Autobiographia Religioso" was inspired by Frank O'Hara's poem, *Autobiographia Literaria*.

The *Tewa* are a Native Puebloan people of the American Southwest.

Otro diente is Spanish for "other tooth."

A *kiva* is a round covered pit used by Native American Pueblo peoples for ceremonial purposes.

Biscochitos are traditional New Mexico cookies made with anise seeds, usually served during Christmas.

A *Penitente* is a member of the Penitente Brotherhood, a lay confraternity of Roman Catholics, chiefly in Spanish American communities in northern New Mexico, known for their practice of self-flagellation, especially during Holy Week.

Maize is the Spanish word for corn.

Pontormo—Jacopo da Pontormo (1494–1557) was an Italian Mannerist painter of the Rennaisance who used very vivid colors.

Arroyo is a Spanish word for gully.

In "Namesake," "The Wind Cries Mary" is a song written by Jimi Hendrix.

A *descanso* is a roadside memorial marked with a cross at the site of an accident.

Acknowledgments

As always, special thanks to my husband, Kenneth Apt, and my son, Daniel DeVito, for their unwavering support of my writing.

Thanks to Ioanna Carlsen, Grace Cavalieri, Thomas Centolella, and Ethelbert Miller. To Maggie Smith and Richard Lehnert for editing.

Great appreciation to my brother Greg Morris, my sisters Diane and Kathleen, nurses Anne McConnell and Sheryl Dougherty, Dr. Gloria Ruiz, Dr. Karin Thron, Dr. Diane Friedman, Glenys Carl, Frances, Page, Kayoko, Prema, and all the folks at Coming Home Connection and Amber Care Hospice Center.

Much gratitude to my writing group who see possibilities through rough drafts: Tina Carlson, Deborah Casillas, Robyn Covelli-Hunt, Donald Levering, Gary Worth Moody, and Barbara Rockman.

Thanks to Debbi Brody, Diane Castiglioni, Deanna Einspahr, Jean Fogel Zee, Ginger Legato, Patti Reuss, Zoe Robles, Kathryn Stately, and Sarah Wolbach.

Gracias J. Bruce Fuller for recognizing this manuscript.

I gratefully acknowledge the literary journals where these
poems first appeared, sometimes in slightly different ver-
sions and/or under different titles:

About Place Journal: "Dear January"
Arts & Letters: "Coyote" and "Rumors"
Barrow Street: "Heritage"
Chiron Review: republished "Autobiographia Religioso"
Citron Review: "I Try to Get Out of the Way, So the Soul
   May Draw Near," also nominated for Best MicroFic-
   tion, 2020
Gargoyle: "Namesake"
Gingko Tree Review: "Toulouse-Lautrec, a Café in Paris"
Innisfree: "Autobiographia Religioso"
Manzano Mountain Review: "Easter"
Poet Lore: "Nuevo México"
Rattle: "Dear November"
Santa Fe Telepoem Booth: republished "Deduction" as audio
Southern Humanities Review: "Dear September"
Spillway: "He Says March"
Sugar House Review: "Living at 7,000 Feet"
Superstition Review: "Crone" and "Deduction"